First World War
and Army of Occupation
War Diary
France, Belgium and Germany

47 DIVISION
Divisional Troops
C Squadron King Edward's Horse
21 April 1915 - 31 May 1916

WO95/2717/1

The Naval & Military Press Ltd
www.nmarchive.com
Published in association with The National Archives

Published by

The Naval & Military Press Ltd

Unit 10 Ridgewood Industrial Park,

Uckfield, East Sussex,

TN22 5QE England

Tel: +44 (0) 1825 749494

www.naval-military-press.com

www.nmarchive.com

This diary has been reprinted in facsimile from the original. Any imperfections are inevitably reproduced and the quality may fall short of modern type and cartographic standards.

© **Crown Copyright**
Images reproduced by permission of The National Archives, London, England, 2015.

Contents

Document type	Place/Title	Date From	Date To
Heading	WO95/2717 Apr 15-May 16 'C' Squadron King Edward's Horse		
Heading	47th Division 'C' Squadn King Edwards Horse 21.4 1-8-15		
War Diary		21/04/1915	25/04/1915
War Diary	Ecquedecques	25/04/1915	06/05/1915
War Diary	Beuvry	07/05/1915	01/08/1915
Heading	47th Division "C" Squadn K.E's Horse (47th Div Cas) Vol II From 2-31.8.15		
War Diary		02/08/1915	31/08/1915
Heading	47th Division "C" Squadn King Edwards Horse Vol III Sept 15		
War Diary		01/09/1915	30/09/1915
Heading	47th Division C Squadron King Edwards Horse (47th Divl Cavy) Vol IV Oct 15		
War Diary		01/10/1915	31/10/1915
Heading	47th Division "C" Sq K.E Horse Nov Vol V		
War Diary		01/11/1915	30/11/1915
Heading	47th Div "C" Sqd K.Edwards Horse Dec Vol V		
War Diary	Hurionville	01/12/1915	01/12/1915
War Diary	Ligne	02/12/1915	02/12/1915
War Diary	Hurionville	03/12/1915	14/12/1915
War Diary	Drouvin	15/12/1915	18/12/1915
War Diary	Vaudricourt	19/12/1915	31/12/1915
War Diary	Drouvin	01/01/1916	31/01/1916
Miscellaneous	D.A.G 3rd Echelon	01/03/1916	01/03/1916
War Diary	Drouvin	01/02/1916	14/02/1916
War Diary	Hurionville	15/02/1916	28/02/1916
Miscellaneous	Hurionville	16/02/1916	16/02/1916
Miscellaneous	D.A.G 3rd Echelon Base	05/04/1916	05/04/1916
War Diary	Hurionville	01/03/1916	06/03/1916
War Diary	Marthes	07/03/1916	09/03/1916
War Diary	Bruay	10/03/1916	13/03/1916
War Diary	Magnicourt	14/03/1916	20/03/1916
War Diary	Hermin	21/03/1916	31/03/1916
Miscellaneous	D.A.G 3rd Echelon Base	02/05/1916	02/05/1916
War Diary	Hermin	01/04/1916	11/05/1916
War Diary	Carly	12/05/1916	29/05/1916
War Diary	Reclinghem	30/05/1916	30/05/1916
War Diary	Valhuon	31/05/1916	31/05/1916

WO95/2717

Apr 15 – May 16   'C' Squadron
King Edward's Horse

47th Warwicks

121/6357

Captain Knightbread's case
Vol I
21.4. 1 - 8 - 15

Apr 15
May 16

War — Diary of "C" Squadron King Edward's Horse

Date & Place	Summary of events & information	Remarks and references to Appendices
April 21	**BISHOPS STORTFORD** Left in two trains at 7-30 & 9-10 a.m. **SOUTHAMPTON.** Arrived at 1 pm & 3 pm respectively. Exchanged 4 riding & one L.D. horses with "Remounts" at the docks.	E.W.H.
7-30 p.m.	Left in company with "B" Squadron, & a few details of men & horses of other units, in Hired Transport No. 0182. "Palm Branch" Major E. W. Hermon in command of the ship.	
April 22 7-30 am	Arrived at HAVRE — Very good passage.	

April 22nd	Escorted across by two destroyers. No submarine scares.
7-0 am.	Commenced to dis-embark.
8-15 ..	Completed disembarkation without accident.
Noon	Arrived at No 6 LARGE REST CAMP.
April 23rd 11 a.m.	Received orders to entrain at No 3 Point GARE des MARCHANDISES at 18h 30 mins.
10-25 pm.	Left HAVRE in one train; B Squadron having entrained & left some two hours earlier.
April 24 4 am.	Halted at MONTEROULIER BOUCHEY for watering the horses & coffee & handy for men
11 am	ditto at ABBEVILLE — & from here went via the outskirts of BOULOGNE & CALAIS to HAZEBROUCK where we received orders to detrain at LILLERS. It was here we first heard the guns in action
10-30 pm	Arrived at LILLERS, raining hard & detrained at once. Acetylene flares of the greatest assistance, which was more than R.T.O. was, who invaded the trucks with an army of ruffians & threw the saddlery all over the place & it took hours to sort it in the dark while he went off to bed.
April 25 3 am ECQUEDECQUES.	Got settled into a barn full of straw

E.W.H.
E.W.H.
E.W.H.

5 a.m.	leaving the horses linked outside until daylight came. Started getting into billets which was successfully accomplished by afternoon.	
April 26.	G.O.C. visited us.	EWH
April 27 9 a.m.	Left ECQUEDECQUES and marched to FONTINELLE FARM, 3k 5 W. of BETHUNE	EWH
April 28.	Exercised squadron. G.O.C.'s inspection	EWH
April 29.	Reconnaisance scheme to VAUDRICOURT	EWH
April 30.	Dismounted attack practice by Troops Fired firing by sections. Targets roofing tiles: Distance 250 yds % of hits 16.4. — 80 men fired. 5 rounds each. 1 section knocked down all six targets with 22 rounds.	
May 1st	Reconnaisance scheme to CLARENCE RIVER. Section cooking at midday.	EWH
May 2nd.	Squadron paraded 10-15 a.m. for Church Parade	EWH

May 3rd	Squadron Parade at 9 a.m. for Field Firing: Troop Scheme Targets: Roofing tiles 12"x8"– 5 Rounds per man. 56 men fired Range: 350 yds. 14 Targets Squadron %. 17.4.
May 4th	Route march.
May 5th	Exercise early: Rest of day spent cleaning out manure from Farm.
May 6	Same as yesterday
May 7th BEUVRY	The O.C. & 2nd & 3rd Troops ordered to proceed to BEUVRY to arrive there 6 p.m. Billeted on arrival: 1st & 4th Troops detailed as Corps Troops 1st Corps remained at FONTINELLE awaiting orders under command of Lieut. B. H. Barker.
May 8th	1 & 4th Troops remained at Fontinelle 2 & 3 " stood by in BEUVRY.
May 9th	1 & 4 Troops proceeded to LE TOURET & LOCON respectively for the purpose of escorting German Prisoners. Arrived 5-30 a.m. 2 & 3 Troops rendezvoused in a

Signatures: EWSt (repeated in right margin)

wood half way to LE QUESNOY. in divisional reserve during the attack by 1st Army on the line RUE DU BOIS — FESTUBERT. Stayed there until after dark when returned to BEUVRY. See attached A.F. C 2123. G.H. 624 – et seq.

Ref: Maps 1/40,000 BETHUNE See Operation Orders Nos. 5 - 6, G.T. 664

Not attached EWH

May 10th. 1 & 4 Troops exchanged places on in evening concentrated at LOCON. Marched out early to same place as yesterday & remained in constant readiness throughout the day. Billeted at LE QUESNOY in the evening. Transport etc coming on from BEUVRY.

EWH

May 11th. Exercise for both ½ squadrons

EWH

May 12th. Ditto

EWH

" 13" Ditto : 1 & 4 Troops to CHOCQUES.

EWH

" 14th " 1 & 4 Troops rejoined the squadron at LE QUESNOY

EWH

" 15 Exercise : Saddled up at 11-30pm remained in a state of constant readiness all night

EWH

May 16th	Remained in constant readiness up to midday.	See Operation orders No 7 – 8 – 9. Instructions a/49 G.H. 838-86. Ends
May 17th	Readiness 1 hour.	GB – 992-5. Ends
May 18th	Readiness 2 hours	G.T. – 90. 93.
May 19th	–do– Shells intended for French observation balloon fell very close to our horse lines	
May 20th	Readiness 2 hours.	
May 21st	–do–	
May 22nd	–do–	
May 23rd	–do– Church parade 10 A.M.	
May 24th	Readiness 1 hour. Attack on ~~Fetubert~~ FESTUBERT-GIVENCHY front by 47th (LONDON) Division, attack successful. 10.30 p.m. 3rd troop proceeded to LE PREOL and escorted about 30 prisoners to CHOQUES. 11 p.m. 2nd troop ordered to patrol in rear of firing line to collect battle stragglers	
May 25	Readiness 1 hour	
May 26	" 1 hour	

May 27th	Readiness 2 hours. Squadron bombing class 2.30 pm. 2 N.C.Os per troop
May 28th	— do —
May 29th	— do —
May 30th	— do — Church parade. 10 AM.
May 31st	— do —
June 1st	Squadron moved to new billet at VAUDRICOURT CHATEAU. Moved one troop at a time to avoid attracting attention of enemy. 4th troop left LE QUESNOY at 2 pm, 1st troop 2.45 pm, 3rd troop 3.30 pm & 2nd troop 4.15 pm. Men bivouacked
June 2nd	Readiness 2 hours. Squadron exercise by troops
" 3rd	— do —
" 4th	— do —
" 5th	— do —
" 6th	Church parade 10 AM.
" 7th	Squadron moved to new billet CHAMP DES COURSES HESDIGNEUL.

June 8th	Squadron exercise. Men employed erecting bivouacs during afternoon	
June 9th	Squadron exercise.	
" 10th	Reconnaissance scheme & troops moving by parallel routes & maintaining touch with each other & the main body by mounted messengers	
" 11th.	Squadron exercise	
" 12th	— do —. Reconnaissance of advanced second line by OC & troop leaders.	See Operation orders. G/216/
" 13th.	Squadron parade 9 A.M. Troop training 1 hr. Squadron drill 1 hr.	
" 14th	Ditto — Constant readiness from 4 pm.	
" 15th	Readiness 1 hr. Squadron exercise	
" 16	— do — readiness ½ hr from 8 pm in anticipation of German counter attack from the direction of LOOS which did not materialize	
" 17th	Readiness 1 hour.	
" 18	— do — Squadron parade 9 A.M. Troop training 1 hr. Squadron drill 1 hr.	

June 19th	Squadron exercise
June 20th	Return to normal readiness of 2 hours. Squadron parade 9 AM
June 21st	T/O.
June 22nd	Squadron exercise. 2nd troop went into trenches for 48 hours from tonight for instructional purposes. Left camp 7 pm rode to NOEUX LES MINES and marched from there to trenches in front of MAROC occupied by 19th T/Att LONDON REGT
June 23rd	Squadron exercise
" 24th	-do- 2nd troop returned from trenches & replaced by 3rd troop no casualties
" 25th	Squadron exercise
" 26	-do- 3rd troop returned from trenches & replaced by 4th troop no casualties
" 27	Squadron exercise
" 28th	-do- 4th troop returned from trenches & replaced by 1st troop no casualties
" 29	Squadron exercise. Reinforcement of 8 men arrived.

June 30th	Squadron exercise 1st troop returned from trenches no casualties. 2nd Lt the Hon H.S Fielding slightly injured in accident at the Divisional Bomb school & admitted to hospital.	
July 1st.	Squadron exercise. 1 Officer & 23 men to Thienne to draw remounts for Division	
July 2nd	Squadron exercise	
" 3rd	- do -	
" 4th	- do - Message from G.O.C with favourable report on conduct of troops while in trenches	
" 5th	- do - 2nd Lt. Fielding returned to duty	
" 6th	- do - 1 Officer & 10 men to Bethune to draw remounts for division	
" 7th	Squadron exercise	
" 8th	Squadron parade 10.30 AM drill order for inspection by LORD KITCHENER	
" 9th	Squadron exercise	
" 10th	- do - visited by Officers of "B" Squadron who are now at BURBURE	
" 11th	Church parade 10.30 AM	

July 12th	Squadron exercise. Squadron sports in evening interrupted by orders received at 6.30pm to send party consisting of 1 Officer 3 NCOs + 15 men to take over traffic control posts at MARLES LES MINES from 48th Division	
July 13th	Squadron exercise	
July 14th	" Controls at MARLES LES MINES taken over by 48th Division.	
July 15th	Squadron exercise, completed squadron sports in evening.	
July 16th	Squadron exercise, control posts at MARLES LES MINES again taken over by us.	
" 17	Squadron exercise	
" 18	Church parade 10 AM. O.C accompanied by S.S.M & 2nd Lt T.D. Stevenson reconnoitred approaches to the French line on the right of 47th Division	See Operation orders. G/216/29
" 19	Squadron exercise	
" 20th	-do- Controls at MARLES LES MINES taken over by 15th Division which has replaced 48th Division	
" 21st	Squadron exercise	

July 22nd	Squadron exercise	
" 23rd	—do—	
" 24th	—do—	
" 25th	Church parade 10 AM	
" 26th	Squadron exercise	
" 27th	—do—	
" 28th	—do—	
" 29th	Squadron exercise under orderly Officer before breakfast remainder of day general fatigue clearing site for new camp in MOISTES MAMES where we have received orders to move on 2nd prox. Erected Dam to conserve water for horses & opened up spring giving sufficient pure water for mens drinking & cooking purposes.	
" 30th	Squadron exercise under orderly officer as yesterday & rest of day given to further preparation of new Camp site.	
31st	—Do—	
Aug 1st	Voluntary Communion service 7 AM.	

47th Division

121/6587.

"C" Squad'n R.E's Horse (47th Divl. Cav.)

from 2 - 31. 8. 15

August 2nd	Squadron moved from Camp at HESDIGNEUL to new camp in BOIS DES DAMES. Left HESDIGNEUL 7 A.M. Division now resting and the squadron on 4 hours notice
August 3rd	Squadron exercise 6.30 A.M. Remainder of day men on general fatigue erecting bivouacs making cook houses etc
August 4th	Squadron exercise
August 5th	— do —
August 6th	Squadron parade 8.30 A.M. map-reading scheme. Officers at LOZINGHEM, ALLOUAGNE, PONT DU REVEILLION & in the BOIS DU MAROQUET. SECTIONS sent off at 5 minute intervals to visit each post in turn.
August 7th	Squadron parade 8.30 A.M. Reconnaissance scheme 3rd Troop as enemy. Bombing class in afternoon.
August 8th	Church parade 11 A.M.
August 9th	Troop training parade 8.30 A.M. Sports of 7th (LONDON) Brigade R.F.A. in afternoon at HESDIGNEUL. 2nd Lt Hon H.S. Feilding 3rd in officers open jumping. Lce Cpl Henderson 1st & S.S.M Stewart 3rd in N.C.Os & Mens open jumping.

August 10	Bathing parade 8.30 AM.
August 11	Squadron exercise 8.30 AM
August 12	Squadron parade 8.45 AM. Squadron took up line of observation posts watching the crossings of the CLARENCE RIVER, reports written by section leaders on all movements of troops observed.
August 13	Troop training, parade 8.45 AM, training men & horses, with the object of attaining greater handiness
August 14	Troop training continued
August 15	— do —
August 16	Church parade 11 AM
August 17	Sqdn exercise 8.30 AM inoculation of men who were inoculated on mobilisation
August 18	Sqdn exercise 8.30 AM
August 19	Troop training as for 13th 14th & 15th inst.
August 20	— do —

August 21st	Bathing parade 8.30 AM.
August 22nd	Church parade 11.30 AM. 2nd Troop left camp 9 AM to take over control posts at MARLES LES MINES.
August 23rd	Squadron exercise 8.30 AM
August 24	—do— Large fatigue party to ALLOUAGNE to prepare ground for divisional sports
August 25	Divisional Sports at ALLOUAGNE. Major E. V. Vernon won officers jumping competition & the squadron also secured the following prizes 1st & 2nd best light draught horse, 2nd for best turned out limbered waggon, spans of mules, 2nd tug of war, 3rd NCOs & men's jumping competition, 3rd high jump, 3, 1/4 mile.
August 26	Troop training as before at 8.30 AM. Second inoculation in evening
August 27	Sqdn exercise 8.30 AM. Took over traffic control post at ROUVIN 1 N.C.O & 4 men.
August 28	Troop training 8.30 AM practice in the use of the sword mounted.
August 29	Sqdn parade 8.30 AM Squadron proceeded to NOEUX LES MINES where it was employed digging trenches for the use of the divisional trench school.

August 30th	Squadron parade 8.45 AM Squadron employed as yesterday
August 31st	-Do- 2/Lt Hon H.S. Feilding left the Squadron to become 1st A.D.C. to G.O.C. 2nd Division.

47th Division

121/7100

"C" Squad" King Edwards Horse.

Vol III

Sept 15

27.10.15

September 1st	Squadron Battery parade 8.30 A.M.
September 2nd	Squadron exercise
" 3rd	— do —
" 4th	Squadron parade 10 AM full marching order. 110 men to FOUQUEREIL in afternoon to determine respects
" 5th	No church parade.
" 6th	Squadron parade & scheme 8.45 AM. Party engaged preparing traffic notes from new divisional refilling point at HAILLICOURT to front line at MAROC. Note With reference to establishment of a squadron on active service, no allowance is made for men acting as second waggon men, with the present establishment of waggons 6 men are thus employed for whom horses are provided, as these men cannot perform their squadron duties it is a question whether the establishment of horses should not be reduced by the number?
" 7th	Squadron exercise 8.30 AM. Party employed as yesterday. Control post at TROUVIN taken over by Divisional Cyclist Co 10 AM. Patrols on new traffic route 9 P.M. till 2 AM 8th inst
" 8th	Squadron exercise 8.30 AM. Patrols on traffic routes at night as yesterday.

September 9th	Squadron moved from BOIS DES DAMES to HAILLICOURT starting 3.30 p.m. Men billeted in school with exception of 1 troop for whom no billet could be found & which therefore continued to bivouac	
Sept 10th	Squadron paraded 7AM & proceeded to MAZINGARBE where it was employed digging communication trenches. Road patrols on traffic routes at night.	
Sept 11th	Squadron parade 7AM & employed as yesterday.	
Sept 12th	Squadron parade 7AM & employed as yesterday	
Sept 13th	Squadron parade 7AM & employed as yesterday	
Sept 14th	– do –	
Sept 15th	– do –	
Sept 16th	– do –	
Sept 17th	Squadron parade 7 AM & employed as before. ~~Communication trench completed and orders received as follows from C.O.C.~~	See 21st inst
Sept 18th	Squadron parade 7AM & employed as before. Party employed at 9 P.M. 4 officers & 30 men picketting roads and as guides to ensure the safe conduct of waggons of Divisional Ammunition Column containing gas cylinders	

Sept 18th (continued)	from detraining point at VERQUIN to unloading point behind front line trenches at MAROC. 36 waggons passed through & unloaded by 1 AM without accident or casualty.
Sept 19th	Party engaged after dark passing up waggons as last night, 3 officers and 3 N.C.Os only employed as guides, as picquets were found unnecessary
Sept 20th	T/reft of 5 OR & 9 horses received
Sept 21st	Squadron parade 7 AM Squadron completed communication trench. Telegram received from G.O.C as follows "The G.O.C directs me to communicate to you his appreciation of the excellent way in which the entrenching work called for from your squadron has been carried out — The C.R.E reports upon the work & methods as exceptionally good — please inform all ranks" — Ends.
Sept 22nd	Squadron again digging on a special trench by request of C.R.E work considerably hindered by enemy shelling.
Sept 23rd	Matting parade 9 a.m.

Sept 24th	Squadron moved 6 pm to battle position at prisoners depôt at "Smelly Farm" midway between NOEUX LES MINES & LES BREBIS. Party of 1 officer & eight men to LES BREBIS to act as prisoners escort.
Sept 25	Attack 6.30 A.M. by 1st Army capturing LOOS about 2000 prisoners & much material. Squadron employed escorting prisoners & guarding prisoners depôt.
Sept 26	Squadron employed as yesterday prisoners still coming through in small batches
Sept 27	— do —
Sept 28	— do —
Sept 29	Major E. V. Sherman, Lieut MacKinnon & 6 men to LOOS to remove captured guns & material, one man slightly wounded. Transport horses to LOOS to remove abandoned transport but shellholes in LOOS made this impossible
Sept 30	Squadron paraded 5 pm rode to MAROC & marched to LOOS & continued removal of material, shells, rifles, bombs etc. No casualties.

47th Division 121/7400

(Spray on lines forward Hrd
at 41st Hrd Levy)
pc IV -
Oct 15

47th Division

121/7400

(Squadron King Edwards Horse
(17th Divl Cavy)

Vol IV

Oct 15

October	1st	Squadron moved to bivouac at GOSNAY 11 AM.
"	2nd	~~Church parade 11.30 AM~~ Resting and cleaning
"	3rd	Church parade 11.30 AM
"	4th	Squadron moved to billets in CHARTREUSE. Squadron fatigue in afternoon in order to make billets habitable.
"	5th	Squadron under orders to move at short notice and remained so all day.
"	6th	11 AM moved back to old billets at HAILLICOURT. Afternoon squadron fatigue to make place habitable as it had been left in a filthy condition by the troops occupying it since the Squadron left.
"	7th	Exercise 9 AM. In the afternoon a Rugby Football match against the 32nd Regiment of Infantry of the French Army.
"	8th	Matting parades at 8.30 AM and 2 PM. Squadron at 1/2 hrs notice from 6 pm until morning owing to German attack.
"	9th	Divisional Parade for inspection by General Rawlinson G.O.C 4th Corps, who congratulated the Division upon its share in the attack on Loos.

October 10	Voluntary Church parade
October 11	2.p.m moved to billets at NOEUX LES MINES
October 12	Squadron fatigue to clean billets & make them fit to live in. Squadron at ½ hrs notice from 6 p.m
October 13	Still on ½ hrs notice
" 14	— do —
" 15	Bathing parade
" 16	Squadron exercise
" 17	Church parade 11 A.M
" 18	Missing benches for Divisional Bomb School
" 19	— do —
" 20	— do —
" 21	— do —
" 22	— do —
" 23	— do —

October 4	Church parade
October 25	Heavy continuous rain all day converting horse lines into a sea of sticky mud
October 26	Draft of 1 sergeant & 9 men received. Party of 1 officer & 28 OR paraded 6 pm & proceeded to work at LENS ROAD REDOUBT returning 2 AM
October 27	Squadron exercise
October 28	Visit of His Majesty the King; 50 men of squadron employed policing route. Appearance of party highly creditable considering the conditions of mud & wet. Digging party as for 26th inst at LENS ROAD REDOUBT.
October 29	Squadron exercise & digging party as yesterday
October 30	— do —
Oct 31st	— do —

17th K warin

November 1st	Party of 1 officer & 20 men engaged digging redoubt in old German second line on LENS ROAD. Party paraded 4.30 pm commenced digging 6.30 pm.	
November 2nd	Digging party as yesterday	
November 3	— do —	
November 4	— do —	
November 5	— do — fairly heavy shelling	
November 6	— do — shelling continued no casualties but squadron stretcher badly shaped.	
" 7	— do — still shelling	
" 8	— do — decided decrease in shelling	
" 9	— do —	
" 10	— do —	

November 10	Squadron horse lines moved to higher ground owing to the continuous rain & consequent mud. Digging impossible
November 11.	Digging party as before but unable to continue working owing to weather.
November 12.	– do –
November 13.	Squadron engaged clearing up lines & billets preparatory to moving back to rest.
November 14.	Squadron moved to billets at HURION-VILLE. Party of 1 Officer & 10 men to Divisional bomb school.
November 15.	Squadron exercise
November 16.	Squadron scheme conducting convoy.
November 17.	Squadron commenced construction of brick horse standings
November 18.	Squadron exercise & continuation of work on standings
November 19.	– do –

November 20.	Squadron exercise & continued work on horse standings
November 21st	Church parade
November 22nd	Squadron exercise & continued work on horse standings
November 23rd	— do —
November 24	— do —
November 25	— do —
November 26	— do —
November 27	— do —
November 28	Bathing parade & continued bricking
November 29	Squadron exercise &; work on horse standings stopped by severe frost.
November 30	Continued work & on brick standings

"C" Sqdn. K. Edwards Horse
Dec & Jan
Vol VII
V.I

WAR DIARY
or
~~INTELLIGENCE SUMMARY~~

(Erase heading not required.)

Army Form C. 2118

Instructions regarding War Diaries and Intelligence Summaries are contained in F. S. Regs., Part II. and the Staff Manual respectively. Title Pages will be prepared in manuscript.

Place	Date	Hour	Summary of Events and Information	Remarks and references to Appendices
HURIONVILLE	1/12/15	6AM	Divisional Route March. Squadron Parade. Squadron acting as cavalry of the advanced guard, forming up on that line or conclusion of march until relieved by infantry. Filled to night at LIGNE	
LIGNE	2/12/15	5.30AM	Squadron Parade. Squadron employed as yesterday on return march to billets at HURIONVILLE	
HURIONVILLE	3/12/15	9.15AM	Squadron Horse lines moved owing to heavy rain rendering old standing untenable. Horses mostly slit under cover in barns etc. Unable to continue construction of lines standing as A.S.C. could furnish no waggons.	
"	4/12/15	9.15AM	"	
"	5/12/15	"	"	
"	6/12/15	"	"	
"	7/12/15	"	"	

Army Form C. 2118

WAR DIARY
or
INTELLIGENCE SUMMARY
(Erase heading not required.)

Instructions regarding War Diaries and Intelligence Summaries are contained in F. S. Regs., Part II. and the Staff Manual respectively. Title Pages will be prepared in manuscript.

Place	Date	Hour	Summary of Events and Information	Remarks and references to Appendices
HURIONVILLE	8/11/15	9.15AM 2/pm	Squadron exercise. Continued work on trench line standing	
"	9/11/15	-	— do —	
"	10/11/15	-	— do —	
"	11/11/15	-	Trench standing completed	
"	12/11/15	-	Squadron exercise	
"	13/11/15	"	— do —	
"	14/11/15	"	— do —	
PROUVIN.	15/11/15	9AM	Squadron moved to HQ at PROUVIN CHATEAU. On arrival received orders to move to VAUDRICOURT to make room for Headquarters of 16th Division from England. These orders were subsequently cancelled & squadron remained at Chateau.	

Army Form C. 2118

WAR DIARY
or
INTELLIGENCE SUMMARY
(Erase heading not required.)

Instructions regarding War Diaries and Intelligence Summaries are contained in F. S. Regs., Part II. and the Staff Manual respectively. Title Pages will be prepared in manuscript.

Place	Date	Hour	Summary of Events and Information	Remarks and references to Appendices
Trouvin	16/1/15	9.15 AM	Squadron Exercise. Exercising Squadron very difficult in the very bad road, as all main roads are strewn to exercising horses a side tracks are knee deep in mud.	
"	17/1/15	"	Squadron Exercise. Orders received to move squadron to VAUDRICOURT on 19 inst	
"	18/1/15	"	Squadron Exercise	
		2 pm	Squadron Commanders given to helping Row Punces in new billeting Area	
VAUDRICOURT	19/1/15		Squadron moved to billets at VAUDRICOURT. The men & horses hat to new lines prepared yesterday men were marched over phones about 1/4 mile	
"	20/1/15	9.15 AM	Exercise	
	21st	"	— do —	

WAR DIARY
or
INTELLIGENCE SUMMARY
(Erase heading not required.)

Army Form C. 2118

Place	Date	Hour	Summary of Events and Information	Remarks and references to Appendices
VAUDRICOURT	23/12/15	9.15 AM	Commenced building stabling. Timber to support length grooms & filled squared timber to ridge pole, rafters etc drawn from R.E. Truss stables to be each 86' 6" long by 28' broad, 10' high to ridge pole, 4' 6" to eaves, supports every 14' 3". Roofing the sailcloth 30' x 30' drawn from R.E. Ends closed with sailcloth, sides left open.	
"	24		Continued building	
"	25		— do — Christmas day. Squadron dismissed at 11 AM; duties throughout the day by guards midday & evening water fed carried out by officers & sergeants.	
"	26		Continued work on stabling	
"	27		— do — 1st troop moved into stable, which takes a full troop easily leaving ample room for saddlery & forage.	

WAR DIARY
or
INTELLIGENCE SUMMARY

(Erase heading not required.)

Army Form C. 2118

Place	Date	Hour	Summary of Events and Information	Remarks and references to Appendices
VAUDRICOURT	28/11/15		4th Tn/p moved into stable. Horses [up?] to present left standing in [open?] [unreadable]	
"	29/11/15		3rd Tn/p moved into stable	
"	30		2nd Tn/p moved into stable. Stables constructed in order of seniority of Tn/ps. Leaders Odd [Numb?] Horses now in Stables. Work commenced on Stable for remaining Horses.	
"	31st		Working on Remainder stable	

WAR DIARY
or
INTELLIGENCE SUMMARY
(Erase heading not required.)

Army Form C. 2118

Instructions regarding War Diaries and Intelligence Summaries are contained in F.S. Regs., Part II. and the Staff Manual respectively. Title Pages will be prepared in manuscript.

Place	Date	Hour	Summary of Events and Information	Remarks and references to Appendices
DROUVIN	1/1/16	9.15am	Exercise. Stables completed to transport & they moved in them getting all horses under cover. Party of 1 SSt + 8 men sent up to a Divisional Sheepskin stores	
"	2/1/16	"	Sunday	
"	3/1/16	"	—do—	
"	4/1/16	"	—do—	
"	5/1/16	"	—do—	
"	6/1/16	"	Messrs Willet moved from VAUDRICOURT to DROUVIN CHATEAU. Squadron Headquarters moved back to DROUVIN CHATEAU	
"	7/1/16	9.15am	Exercise	
"	8/1/16	"	—do—	
"	9/1/16	10am	Church parade	

WAR DIARY
or
INTELLIGENCE SUMMARY

Army Form C. 2118

(Erase heading not required.)

Instructions regarding War Diaries and Intelligence Summaries are contained in F.S. Regs., Part II. and the Staff Manual respectively. Title Pages will be prepared in manuscript.

Place	Date	Hour	Summary of Events and Information	Remarks and references to Appendices
DROUVIN	10/1/16	9.15 AM	Exercise Draft of 50 OR arrived from Base.	
"	11/1/16		Exercise	
"	12/1/16		—do—	
"	13/1/16		—do— Shrapnel shell down two Billet Estany	
"	14/1/16	6.30 PM	—do— Report received from Shrapnel who reports Sergt Macaulay killed in action by shell	
"	15/1/16	9.15 AM	Batt. parade.	
"	16/1/16	10 AM	Church parade.	
"		1 PM	Report received from Shrapnel who reports Th Mackin killed in action by shell	
"	17/1/16		Exercise	
"	18/1/16		"	

WAR DIARY
or
INTELLIGENCE SUMMARY

Army Form C. 2118

(Erase heading not required.)

Instructions regarding War Diaries and Intelligence Summaries are contained in F.S. Regs., Part II. and the Staff Manual respectively. Title Pages will be prepared in manuscript.

Place	Date	Hour	Summary of Events and Information	Remarks and references to Appendices
TROUVIN	19/1/16	9.15am	Exercise	
"	20/1/16	10am	Squadron parade to watch Father Xmas between FERFAY and LILLERS during passing of General JOFFRE.	
"	21/1/16	9.am	Bathing parade at Mine at BRUAY	
"	22/1/16		- do -	
"	23/1/16	10am	Church Parade.	
"	24/1/16	9am	Musketry at CHAMP DE TIR LABEUVRIERE. Rapid fire practice by Erskine. Exercise	
"	25/1/16			
"	26/1/16	9am	Musketry as for 24th inst.	
"	27/1/16		Exercise	

WAR DIARY
or
INTELLIGENCE SUMMARY

Army Form C. 2118

Instructions regarding War Diaries and Intelligence Summaries are contained in F. S. Regs., Part II. and the Staff Manual respectively. Title Pages will be prepared in manuscript.

(Erase heading not required.)

Place	Date	Hour	Summary of Events and Information	Remarks and references to Appendices
DROUVIN	28/1/16	9 AM	Battn parade & Divine Service at DROUVIN	
"	29/1/16		— do —	
"	30/1/16	10 AM	Church parade. Major Denman a 2nd Lts Tullok & Syme to attend 1 weeks course at 9 Corps school for killers. Major Denman as instructor. Remainder mounted troops.	
"	31/1/16	9 AM	Musketry. Individual practice for men who though going to hospital on other causes have only maximally shot with the rifle now in their possession.	

1875 Wt. W593/826 1,000,000 4/15 J.B.C. & A. A.D.S.S./Forms/C. 2118.

To.
D. A. G.
   3rd Echelon
       Base

Herewith please find war diary of "C" Squadron King Edward's Horse for the month of February 1916.

March 1st 1916.

E W Sherman **MAJOR.,**
COMMANDING "C" SQUADRON,
KING EDWARD'S HORSE.

Jan & Feb /16

Army Form C. 2118

WAR DIARY
or
INTELLIGENCE SUMMARY
(Erase heading not required.)

Instructions regarding War Diaries and Intelligence Summaries are contained in F. S. Regs., Part II. and the Staff Manual respectively. Title Pages will be prepared in manuscript.

Place	Date	Hour	Summary of Events and Information	Remarks and references to Appendices
PROUVIN	1/2/16	9.15AM	Squadron exercise	
"	2/2/16	"	— do —	
"	3/2/16	"	— do —	
"	4/2/16	"	— do — & troop training for men not required to lead horses	
"	5/2/16	"	— do —	
"	6/2/16	11AM	Church parade. Major E. W. Hermon & 2 Lt Tulloch & Syme returned from	
"	7/2/16	8.15AM	Divisional Riding School	
"	8/2/16	"	Battling parade, ride to mine baths at BRUAY	
"	9/2/16	9.15AM	Squadron exercise	
"	10/2/16	"	— do —	
"	11/2/16	"	— do —	
"	12/2/16	"	— do —	
"	13/2/16	10AM	Church parade	

WAR DIARY
or
INTELLIGENCE SUMMARY
(Erase heading not required.)

Army Form C. 2118

Place	Date	Hour	Summary of Events and Information	Remarks and references to Appendices
DROUVIN	14/2/16	9.15AM	Squadron exercise. Squadron snipers returned from time in trenches for move into rest billets.	
HURIONVILLE	15/2	8.30AM	Squadron moved to rest billets at HURIONVILLE. Pack standings laid during last rest period have lasted well, but head ropes were erected subsequently by other Divisional Cavalry not very satisfactory	
"	16/2	"	Settling into billets	
"	17/2	9 AM	Individual training by troops under troop leaders. Reveille put back to 6 AM	
"	18/2	"	— do —	
"	19/2	"	Continued individual training	
"	20/2	10 AM	Church parade. Lecture in afternoon by O.C. Squadron to O.C. Divisional Mounted troops to officers & NCO's of Squadron & Cyclist Company, on training imposed during period of rest.	
"	21/2	9 AM	Advance guard scheme to ESTRÉE BLANCHE in conjunction with Cyclist Company	mob HAZEBROUCK 5A

WAR DIARY
or
INTELLIGENCE SUMMARY

(Erase heading not required.)

Place	Date	Hour	Summary of Events and Information	Remarks and references to Appendices
HURIONVILLE	22/2/16	9 AM	Individual training under troop leaders for 1st, 2nd & 3rd troops. 4th troop attached to 142nd Infantry Brigade marching from AUCHY AU BOIS to GUHEM	MEZZ BROUM SA /18000
"	23/2/16	—	Country under snow - training impossible	
"	24/2	—	— do —	
"	25/2	10 AM	— do — 1 Officer & 30 NCOs drawn to LILLERS to detrain remounts 4/or Division	
"	26/2	—	Further snow falls & hard, outdoor operations still at a standstill	
"	27/2/2	10 AM	Church parade. Thaw	
"	28/2	9 AM	Squadron parade. Advance guard to WITTERNESSE followed by outpost Scheme. In conjunction with cyclist Company	

WAR DIARY
or
INTELLIGENCE SUMMARY

Place	Date	Hour	Summary of Events and Information	Remarks and references to Appendices
HURIONVILLE	29/2/16	9 AM	Individual training under troop leaders.	

N.B.

After careful consideration and taking into account that one has to send Stablemen to the A.S.C. to accompany the G.S. wagons also that it is necessary to have stablemen on the limbered wagons I find the following to be the best squadron organisation — i.e reducing the riding horses by six.

P.T.O

Army Form C. 2118

WAR DIARY
or
INTELLIGENCE SUMMARY
(Erase heading not required.)

Instructions regarding War Diaries and Intelligence Summaries are contained in F.S. Regs., Part II. and the Staff Manual respectively. Title Pages will be prepared in manuscript.

Place	Date	Hour	Summary of Events and Information												Remarks and references to Appendices
				N.C.O's & Men					**HORSES**						
				1st Troop	2nd Troop	3rd Troop	4th Troop	Total	1st Troop	2nd Troop	3rd Troop	4th Troop	Total		
HURIONVILLE	6/5/16		S.S.M	1				1				1	1	Officers	TRANSPORT
			S.Q.M.S	1				1				1	1	Riding	6 Horses
			Sergeants	2	2	2	2	8	2	2	2	2	8	Cobs	3 Maltesemen
			Farr Sergeant	1	1		1						–	L.D.	3 Richemoes
			Shoeing Smiths	1	1	2	1	5	2	1	2	–	5	H. T.	with A.S.C. on
			Saddler	1				1				1	1	Mules	3 G.S. Wagons
			Trumpeters	2	2	2	2	8	2	2	2	2	8		
			Corporals	2	2	2	2	8	2	2	2	2	8		
			Trooper	21	21	21	21	84	21	21	21	21	84		
			Batmen	4	4	2	2	12	1				6		
			1st & 2nd divn transport	3	3	3	3	12	{1 interpreter}				1		
				35	33	35	32	135	29	28	30	24	114	Total	152

1873 W¹. W593/326 1,000,000 4/15 J.B.C. & A. A.D.S.S./Forms/C. 2118.

A.G
 3rd Echelon
  Base.

Herewith please find war diary of "C" Sqdn King Edwards Horse for month of March 1916

April 5th 1916

for. MAJOR.,
COMMANDING "C" SQUADRON,
KING EDWARD'S HORSE.

Army Form C. 2118

WAR DIARY
or
INTELLIGENCE SUMMARY
(Erase heading not required.)

Instructions regarding War Diaries and Intelligence Summaries are contained in F. S. Regs., Part II. and the Staff Manual respectively. Title Pages will be prepared in manuscript.

Place	Date	Hour	Summary of Events and Information	Remarks and references to Appendices
HURIONVILLE	1/3/16	9 AM	Individual training under troop leaders.	
	2/3/16	2.15 pm	Musketry	
		9 AM	-Do-. One Officer + two sergeants to Divisional School for instruction in Lewis gun	
"	3/3/16		Heavy snowfall. No outdoor work possible	
"	4/3/16		-do-	
"	5/3/16	10 AM	Church parade	
"	6/3/16	9.15 AM	Squadron exercises	
"	7/3/16	10 AM	Squadron marched from HURIONVILLE to MARTHES on 1st Army training area for 3 days training	
MARTHES			Heavy snowfall. No outdoor work possible	
"	8/3/16		-do-	
"	9/3/16			
"	10/3/16	9 AM	Squadron marched from MARTHES to TRUAY. Owing to R.H. + billets arrangement 2 trps Sqd to billet at one end of TREVAY + 2 trps at the other separated by about a mile.	
TRUAY	11/3/16	9.15 AM	Exercise	

Army Form C. 2118

WAR DIARY
or
INTELLIGENCE SUMMARY
(Erase heading not required.)

Instructions regarding War Diaries and Intelligence Summaries are contained in F. S. Regs., Part II. and the Staff Manual respectively. Title Pages will be prepared in manuscript.

Place	Date	Hour	Summary of Events and Information	Remarks and references to Appendices
BRUAY	12/3/16	10 AM	Church parade	
"	13/3/16	9.15	Squadron exercised under Troop arrangements	
MAGNICOURT	14/3/16	9 AM	Squadron marched from BRUAY to concentrate at MAGNICOURT. Billets at MAGNICOURT	
		12 nun	in very dirty condition. No stabling available for horses so H/r picketed out in lines. Horses taken over to SOUCHEZ/CARENCY sector	
"	15/3/16	9.15 AM	Squadron exercise. Officers employed training details on villages in front. General orders as to billeting capacity.	
"	16/3/16	9.15 AM	— do —	
"	17/3/16		— do — Squadron joined by M.G. section under 2/Lt D.A. Syme, previously attached to "A" Sqdn with 15 Division	
"	18/3/16		— do —	
"	19/3/16	10 AM	Church parade 10 AM	
"	20/3/16	9 AM	Squadron exercise	

Army Form C. 2118

WAR DIARY
or
INTELLIGENCE SUMMARY
(Erase heading not required.)

Instructions regarding War Diaries and Intelligence Summaries are contained in F. S. Regs., Part II. and the Staff Manual respectively. Title Pages will be prepared in manuscript.

Place	Date	Hour	Summary of Events and Information	Remarks and references to Appendices
HERMIN	21/3/16	9.30 AM	Squadron moved to HERMIN. Billets fair to good; stabling accommodation for two troops in shed stalls, remainder in barns.	
"	22/3/16	9 AM	Squadron exercise	
"	23/3/16		— do —	
"	24/3/16		— do — Heavy snow	
"	25/3/16		Party of 20 men & 1 Officer to BOUVIGNY HUTS dismantled for material for maintenance & repair of communication trenches in SOUCHEZ SECTOR.	
"	26/3/16	10 AM	Squadron exercise. Church parade	
"	27/3/16		— do — Commenced construction of stabling to accommodate remainder of squadron & M.G. section	

1875 Wt. W593/826 1,000,000 4/15 J.B.C. & A. A.D.S.S./Forms/C. 2118.

WAR DIARY
or
INTELLIGENCE SUMMARY

(Erase heading not required.)

Army Form C. 2118

Place	Date	Hour	Summary of Events and Information	Remarks and references to Appendices
HERMIN	27/3/16		Continued construction of stablings. Musketry in afternoon	
"	28/3/16		— do —	
"	29/3/16		— do — Squadron dry canteen opened. amuch appreciated by all ranks. Sgt. T. Mackinnon wounded by shrapnel whilst attached to 21st 17th London Regt, a serious loss to the Squadron.	
"	30/3/16		Continued work on stablings. musketry in afternoon.	
"	31/3/16		— do —	

To
D.A.G.
 3rd Echelon.
  Base.

Herewith War Diary of
C. Squadron King Edward's Horse
for month of April 1916.

2/5/16   B.H. Barber, Captain
             for Major
Commanding C. Squadron King Edward's Horse.

Army Form C. 2118

WAR DIARY
or
INTELLIGENCE SUMMARY

(Erase heading not required.)

Instructions regarding War Diaries and Intelligence Summaries are contained in F. S. Regs., Part II. and the Staff Manual respectively. Title Pages will be prepared in manuscript.

Place	Date	Hour	Summary of Events and Information	Remarks and references to Appendices
HERMIN	1/4/16	9.a.m	Squadron Exercise. Trench maintenance party relieved.	
	2/4/16	10.a.m.	Church Parade.	
	3/4/16	9.a.m	Squadron Exercise	
	4/4/16	9.a.m	- do - One half of officers available attended Pecking Coy G.O.C. IV Corps.	
	5/4/16		- do -	
	6/4/16	9.a.m	- do - Major E.W. Herman attached for duty with D.H.Q. 2nd Lt. R.D. Stevenson takes command of the Squadron. 2nd Lt. Strong, machine gun corps attached to Squadron for instruction in horse management.	
	7/4/16	9.a.m	- do -	
	8/4/16	9.a.m	- do - Trench maintenance party relieved. Machine gun section proceeds to GRAND SERVINS be attached to 141st Brigade M.G. Coy. hosiery in the afternoon.	
	9/4/16	10.a.m	Church Parade.	
	10/4/16	10.0.m	Squadron Training.	

1875 Wt. W593/826 1,000,000 4/15 J.B.C. & A. A.D.S.S./Forms/C. 2118.

WAR DIARY
or
INTELLIGENCE SUMMARY

(Erase heading not required.)

Army Form C. 2118

Place	Date	Hour	Summary of Events and Information	Remarks and references to Appendices
HERMIN	11/4/16	9 a.m.	Squadron Exercise.	
	12/4/16	"	— do —	
	13/4/16	"	— do —	
	14/4/16	"	Squadron training	
	15/4/16	"	Squadron Exercise.	
	16/4/16	10 a.m.	Church Parade.	
	17/4/16	9 a.m.	Squadron Exercise — 2nd Lt Spary returns to his unit.	
	18/4/16	"	for patrol duty. 1 N.C.O and 9 men (mounted) sent to report to patrol Post PERNES	
	18/4/16	"	Squadron Exercise.	
	19/4/16	10 a.m.	— do — is full marching order. Capt B.H. Barker returns from 141st Brigade and takes command of Squadron.	
	20/4/16	9 a.m.	Squadron Exercise.	
	21/4/16	"	— do —	
	22/4/16	"	— do —	
	23/4/16			

Army Form C. 2118

WAR DIARY
or
INTELLIGENCE SUMMARY
(Erase heading not required.)

Instructions regarding War Diaries and Intelligence Summaries are contained in F.S. Regs., Part II. and the Staff Manual respectively. Title Pages will be prepared in manuscript.

Place	Date	Hour	Summary of Events and Information	Remarks and references to Appendices
HERMIN	24/9/16	9.a.m.	Squadron Exercises. Patrol post at PERNES relieved.	
	25/9/16	9.a.m.	Squadron training. Musketry in the afternoon.	
	26/9/16	" "	Troop training. Musketry in the afternoon.	
	27/9/16	" "	— do — Musketry in the afternoon.	
	28/9/16	" "	— do — 2nd Lt C.F. Harrison joined the Squadron from the Reserve Squadron.	
	29/9/16	" "	Squadron Exercises.	
	30/9/16	" "	Note. It is suggested that, owing to the fact that the Machine Gun Section is frequently on detached employment, a farrier should be afforded its War Establishment.	

1875 Wt. W593/826 1,000,000 4/15 J.B.C. & A. A.D.S.S./Forms/C. 2118.

WAR DIARY
or
INTELLIGENCE SUMMARY

Army Form C. 2118

O/C K.E. Howe 47

Feb 15

Place	Date	Hour	Summary of Events and Information	Remarks and references to Appendices
HERMIN	1/5/16	9AM	Squadron parade + squadron training marching in afternoon	
"	2/5/16	"	— do —	
"	3/5/16	"	— do —	
"	4/5/16	"	Squadron training	
"	5/5/16	"	Squadron parade full marching order route march	
"	6/5/16	"	Squadron training	
"	7/5/16	"	Major E.W. Herman resumed command of the Squadron. Machine gun section of 1st reserve regiment & orders received for action. Machine guns & horses to rendezvous with M.G. section. Pte Sumerpal killed in action snyling.	
"	8/5/16	9AM	Squadron exercise. S.Q.M.S Alderton accidentally killed by a fall from his horse	
"	9/5/16	"	Preparing for move to join 1st Cavalry Division tomorrow	
"	10/5/16	8AM	Squadron parade inspected by Major Leonard Rn Charles Parker G.O.C. 1st Division before leaving 47 Division. Marched to Vincly via FERFAY midday. Regt FONTAINE LEZ HERMAN billeted night at Vincly	HAZEBROUCK 5A
"	11/5/16	8AM	Squadron marched to CARLY, 2 miles W of SAMER via POURTHES, FAUQUEMBERGUES CAMPAGNE LES BOULONNAIS. To join 1st Cavalry Division for training. Met A Squadron at midday Regt at POURTHES	CALAIS 13

WAR DIARY
or
INTELLIGENCE SUMMARY

(Erase heading not required.)

Army Form C. 2118

Place	Date	Hour	Summary of Events and Information	Remarks and references to Appendices
EARLY	12/5/16		Quiet day to rest. Princes Conference for Officers at H.Q. Corp Mounted Troops School	
"	13/5/16	8.30 AM	Full marching order parade. Short route march	
"	14/5/16		Sunday	
"	15/5/16	"	Officers & N.C.O's lecture by Officer instructor. Men under regular N.C.O's	
		5 pm	Lecture Officers & Sergeants - map reading	
"	16/5/16	8.30 AM	Independent reconnaissance scheme by Squadron & Cyclist Company	
		5 pm	Lecture Protection	
"	17/5/16	8.30 am	Squadron drill on the sea shore at HARDELOT PLAGE	
		4 "	Lecture - Messages	
"	18/5/16	5 AM	Tactical scheme under orders of 1st Cavalry Division	
"	19/5/16	8.30 AM	Advance guard scheme Squadron & Cyclist Company under command of Capt B. St. Barbe.	
		5 pm	Lecture field sketching.	
"	20/5/16	9 AM	Officers lecture at Veterinary Hospital NESLES. Squadron kit parade HARDELOT PLAGE	

Army Form C. 2118

WAR DIARY
or
INTELLIGENCE SUMMARY

(Erase heading not required.)

Instructions regarding War Diaries and Intelligence Summaries are contained in F. S. Regs., Part II. and the Staff Manual respectively. Title Pages will be prepared in manuscript.

Place	Date	Hour	Summary of Events and Information	Remarks and references to Appendices
CARLY	20/5/16		Sunday	
	21/5/16	8.30 AM	Advance guard scheme combination of A & C squadrons & two cyclist companies acting as advance mounted troops to an imaginary Cav of two divisions	
	23/5/16	10 AM	Lecture to officers & sergeants on yesterday's scheme	
		5 pm	" " " - Outlines in open warfare	
	24/5/16	6 AM	Tactical scheme under orders of 1st Cavalry Division. Scheme not very successful from instructional standpoint	
	25/5/16	10 AM	Lecture to officers, patrols	
		11 pm	Night operations. Troops marched separately to rendezvous	
	26/5/16	3 AM	Outpost scheme in conjunction with A squadron & cyclist companies	
		4 AM	Returned to billets	
	27/5/16	8.30 AM	Tactical scheme "C" squadron & 4th Cyclist Co. v "A" Squadron & 12th Div Cyclist Co	
	28/5/16		Sunday	

WAR DIARY
or
INTELLIGENCE SUMMARY

Army Form C. 2118

(Erase heading not required.)

Place	Date	Hour	Summary of Events and Information	Remarks and references to Appendices
CAMLY RECLINGHEM	29/5/16	11 AM	Conference at H.Q. Cavalry Mounted Troops School Hesdin L'ABBÉ	
RECLINGHEM	30/5/16	8 AM	Squadron marched to Willer at RECLINGHEM via CAMPAGNE LEZ BOULONNAIS. "A" Squadron also billeted at RECLINGHEM	
VALHUON	31/5/16	8 AM	Squadron marched to VALHUON to concentrate with "A" & "B" Squadrons to form IV Corps Cavalry Regiment. End of Squadron War Diary	

www.ingramcontent.com/pod-product-compliance
Lightning Source LLC
Chambersburg PA
CBHW081242170426
43191CB00034B/2015